SAFE SEX
in the Age of
AIDS

ABOUT THE FACULTY

ROBERT THEODORE "TED" McILVENNA,
M. Div., Ph.D.
President of The Institute for Advanced Study of Human Sexuality, Theologian, Social Philosopher, Forensic Sexologist. Has worked for the past twenty years designing programs to help people value and understand their sexuality.

WARDELL B. POMEROY, Ph.D.
Dean of American Sexologists, Academic Dean of The Institute for Advanced Study of Human Sexuality, coauthor of *The Kinsey Reports,* author of many publications. One of the pioneers of twentieth century sexology.

LORETTA HAROIAN, Ph.D.
Psychologist, Forensic Sexologist, Dean of Professional Studies at The Institute for Advanced Study of Human Sexuality, Professor of Clinical Sexology. Generally considered one of the leading experts on childhood and adolescent sexuality.

ERWIN J. HAEBERLE, Ph.D., Ed.D.
Professor and Director of Historical Research at The Institute for Advanced Study of Human Sexuality, Cochairman of Scientific Committee, World Congresses of Sexology, 1983 and 1987, Author of *Sex Atlas* and numerous scientific papers. Leading authority on the origins and developments of sexology.

CHARLES MOSER, Ph.D., M.S.W.
Associate Professor of Clinical Sexology at The Institute for Advanced Study of Human Sexuality. One of the new breed of talented scientists specializing in the development of the full range of clinical services from a sexological standpoint.

SAFE SEX
in the Age of
AIDS

Prepared by The Institute for Advanced Study
of Human Sexuality

Citadel Press   Secaucus, New Jersey

10   9   8   7   6   5   4   3   2

Copyright ©1986 by The Institute for Advanced Study
of Human Sexuality

Published by Citadel Press
A division of Lyle Stuart Inc.
120 Enterprise Ave., Secaucus, N.J. 07094
In Canada: Musson Book Company
A division of General Publishing Co. Limited
Don Mills, Ontario

Queries regarding rights and permissions should be addressed to:
Lyle Stuart, 120 Enterprise Avenue, Secaucus, N.J. 07094

Manufactured in the United States of America

ISBN 0-8065-0996-1

Introduction

This is a book about Sexual Management. This is a book about how you can better manage your sexual interest, sexual actions, and sexual negotiations in the "Age of AIDS."

The several authors of this book have tried to be as honest as possible in dealing with what is known and not yet known about Acquired Immune Deficiency Syndrome. The authors are sexologists who know a great deal about human sexual functioning and who have attempted to be as specific as possible in dealing with the relationship between sexual acts and Acquired Immune Deficiency Syndrome.

The responsibility for what you do sexually is ultimately up to you. Sexologists know that regardless of anything else, people will do sexual things. Indeed, the thesis of this book is that we want you to do sexual things, but we want you to consider safe sexual activity.

Contents

A I D S—A Disease and Its Transmission

AIDS (Acquired Immune-Deficiency Syndrome) is the name given to the final and, so far, mostly fatal stage of a viral infection which destroys the body's natural immune system. As a result, patients fall victim to one or several opportunistic infections or may develop tumors, neurological disorders and many other serious health problems. Very often the disease manifests itself in a very dangerous lung infection (*pneumocystis carinii pneumonia*) and/or a form of skin cancer (*Kaposi's sarcoma*), which was formerly quite rare and slow-acting. It then afflicted mostly elderly men, but in AIDS patients it is now rapid and devastating.

The virus responsible for AIDS has been named differently by different researchers (LAV: Montagnier; HTLV-III: Gallo; ARV: Levy), and it seems to have reached the modern, industrialized world only a few years ago. There are some indications that it first appeared in tropical Africa, where by now an enormous number of cases in both men and women have been reported. The virus then seems to have been carried to the Caribbean, the United States, Europe, and the rest of the world. However, this theory is not undisputed. The virus may also be older, or it may have originated somewhere else.

There also seems to be some evidence that an infection with the virus is, by itself, not sufficient to cause AIDS, and that certain other factors (so-called co-factors) must be present, such as a previous weakening of the immune system or some additional, other virus. It has even been suggested that the AIDS virus itself might be nothing more than a co-factor. These and many other questions still await further research.

For example, it is still unclear how many of those infected with the virus will develop AIDS, and if so, when. Moreover, it is by no means certain, only likely, that they will, throughout their lives, remain infectious to others. On the other hand, many of the infected may never develop symptoms, i.e., they may never become sick. Still others may develop a few light or severe symptoms after an indeterminate time. Even so, they may never meet the clinical definition of AIDS.

Such "milder" cases, which can actually be very serious and can even lead to death, are usually called ARC (AIDS-Related Conditions). At the present time, there are no reliable statistics of ARC patients. Many knowledgeable people, however, estimate their number to be about ten times as many as the AIDS cases. Finally, it is estimated that the number of infected individuals without any symptoms is again a hundred times as high as that of the ARC patients. Thus, for every AIDS patient there seem to be about 10 ARC patients and 1000 infected but otherwise healthy men and women.

The first thing to remember, therefore, is this:

PEOPLE DO NOT "CATCH AIDS."

They may "catch" the AIDS virus, which then, over a period of time, may or may not cause AIDS or ARC. At this time, we do not know if or when this will happen to any particular infected person. It will probably happen only to some of the infected, although they may all remain infectious for life, i.e., capable of infecting others.

How people become infected

The AIDS virus has been found in virtually all bodily fluids of infected individuals—blood, semen, vaginal secretions, mother's milk, saliva, urine, feces, even tears. An infection can occur when any of these bodily fluids containing the virus enter the bloodstream of another person. This can happen through direct contact from blood to blood (such as in blood transfusions or the sharing of unsterilized needles among drug users). It can also happen if infected blood from an open wound comes in contact with abrasions, breaks or cuts in the skin of another person. Indeed, such a person with an injured skin can also get infected through external contact with the other already mentioned bodily fluids.

Most of the time, however, people become infected during intimate sexual contact, i.e., when one or several of these bodily fluids are passed from one body to another. Infected semen, particularly, which enters the body during oral, vaginal or anal intercourse may transmit the virus through tiny, often microscopically small internal injuries, of which the people involved remain themselves entirely unaware. This is, of course, also true of infected semen if it is used in artificial insemination.

18

It is still unclear whether the exchange of saliva in deep kissing can, by itself, transmit the virus, but it does not seem impossible, if one of the partners is infected and the other is suffering from bleeding gums. It will probably always be difficult to prove infection through deep kissing, since those who engage in it usually also engage in other forms of physical intimacy. On the other hand, it is clear that the AIDS virus is not transmitted very easily:

PEOPLE CATCH THE AIDS VIRUS ONLY THROUGH VERY INTIMATE PHYSICAL CONTACT.

How people avoid becoming infected

People avoid infection by preventing another person's infected bodily fluids from entering their own bodies. The AIDS virus is too fragile to be transmitted through the air or in any ordinary casual contact. Thus, shaking hands with an infected person, hugging or even dry kissing will not lead to infection. Neither will sharing a workplace or even living in the same household. (However, obviously, one should not share the toothbrushes or razorblades of the infected.)

PEOPLE DO NOT CATCH THE AIDS VIRUS
THROUGH CASUAL SOCIAL CONTACT.

Who is at risk of infection?

All people who allow the bodily fluids of an infected person to enter their own bodies are at risk. Initially, this was especially true of recipients of blood and blood products (in transfusions and as a treatment of hemophilia). At the time, the virus had not yet been identified. Since then, however, the danger has been recognized and eliminated through the testing of all blood donors and the treatment of donated blood.

This now leaves two major modes of transmission:

*   the sharing of contaminated injection needles, and
*   sexual contact.

A third mode is the transmission from a mother to her child before or during birth or through nursing.

We know that, in the Western industrialized societies, the first AIDS cases occurred in homosexual and bisexual men as well as in intravenous drug users. It follows that, for the future, we can define five major risk groups:

PEOPLE AT RISK OF AIDS:

1. Homosexual and bisexual men (keeping in mind that the bisexual men are much more numerous than the exclusively homosexual men).
2. Intravenous drug users sharing needles.
3. The sexual partners of people in these first groups.
4. The sexual partners of these partners.
5. Children conceived, born and nursed by infected mothers.

If we look at this list soberly and objectively, we will have to admit that, potentially, everybody is at risk except those who remain sexually abstinent or live in a truly exclusive sexual relationship.

At this time, the virus has not yet spread very far beyond the original risk groups, and thus the general population, even if sexually active without precautions, is not yet in any immediate danger. However, those who have sexual contact with persons in the risk groups already need to take precautions today. Eventually, all of us may have to do so. In the meantime, we should do everything we can to help all those at risk to protect themselves, because, in the long run, they will thereby also protect everyone else.

PEOPLE AT RISK OF AIDS CAN LEARN TO PROTECT THEMSELVES.

AIDS Prevention

AIDS can be prevented. With the proper precautions, nobody has to catch the AIDS virus. For example, people who receive blood transfusions or blood products are now already protected by the testing of blood donors and the treatment of donated blood. Similarly, intravenous drug users can protect themselves by avoiding the sharing of needles. However, most importantly, infection through sexual contact can be avoided by changes in sexual behavior.

THE NEGATIVE APPROACH

For some the solution is very simple: "Stop having sex! Or never have sex with anyone before or outside marriage!"

Unfortunately, as history and everyday observation show, this advice has never convinced enough people to stop the spread of sexually transmitted diseases anywhere. The advice may be well-intended, quite logical and highly moral, but there is simply no denying the truth that it is ineffective, at least for most people. Neither counseling nor preaching along these lines has ever produced the desired results. Neither promises of heaven nor threats of hell, neither appeals to reason nor draconic punishments have ever produced universal chastity.

The fact of the matter is that many people continue to have sex with each other before and outside of marriage, regardless of religious teachings, criminal law or medical opinion. Posters with skull and bones, pictures of AIDS patients, drastic warnings of all kinds—none of these can be expected to stop sexually transmitted diseases. All of these methods have been tried for hundreds of years and have failed.

THE POSITIVE APPROACH

Sexologists, like all scientists, try to see the world as it is, not as it might be or should be. They then try to come up with some realistic plan of action. In the case of AIDS, this is a change in sexual behavior from "unsafe" to "safe."

Since it is unrealistic to hope for universal sexual abstinence or an immediate, universal formation of permanent, exclusive sexual relationships, it seems more promising to try reducing the risk of infection in the sexual encounters that do take place.

Therefore, instead of emphasizing the negative aspects of "unsafe" sex, sexologists stress the positive aspects of "safe" sex.

Even if sexual patterns have to be changed to prevent infection, they can still lead to satisfaction and complete erotic fulfillment. Indeed, they may even increase communication between partners and thus lead to greater intimacy and mutual understanding.

Men and Women Protecting Each Other—"Safer Sex"

AIDS is, among other things, a sexually transmissible disease. People can catch the AIDS virus during sexual contact, but they can also avoid catching it during sexual contact.

They can protect themselves and each other by practicing "safer sex."

They can change their usual sexual patterns in such a way that the exchange of bodily fluids is avoided.

This may require some effort at first, but it is not all that difficult, if both partners really care for each other and for their own health. Once they start practicing it consistently, they will soon discover: Healthy sex does not have to be dull!

They may even get a real surprise and find that:

> "SAFER SEX" IS BETTER SEX.

THE GUIDELINES

Sexologists have developed some practical guidelines that can help you to reduce the risk of infection with the AIDS virus during sexual contact. Needless to say, if you follow these guidelines, you also reduce the risk of infection with any other sexually transmissible disease. Therefore, the guidelines are a good idea in any case, even without the threat of AIDS.

Basic to these risk reduction guidelines is a close look at all possible sexual behaviors and their division into three major groups:

1. Unsafe.
2. Possibly safe.
3. Safe.

This general grouping can help us to think more objectively about our own various sexual practices and to examine the degree of risk they pose to us and our partners.

The guidelines also help us think about how we can make our sexual lives safer and healthier. We can try to make each of our sexual practices safer in itself or to replace it with another, safer practice.

The guidelines are also a challenge to our imagination. Inventive partners may come up with new, surprising ways of making their own sex lives safe.

In order to get an overall picture of the possibilities, let's begin with a careful, step-by-step examination of the following list:

UNSAFE

"Unsafe" is any sexual practice that can easily transmit the AIDS virus. Such transmission can occur by way of exchanging bodily fluids, especially if, at the same time, there develop small cuts, tears or bruises in the skin or mucous membranes of one or both partners. These injuries can be so microscopically small that they cannot be seen with the naked eye, or they may be internal and invisible for that reason. In any case, they greatly increase the risk of infection.

However, remember that the exchange of bodily fluids alone is already risky. In short:

ANY EXCHANGE OF BODILY FLUID DURING SEX IS UNSAFE.

Even remembering this is not enough, however. It is also quite clear that the unsafe practices become even more unsafe when used repeatedly or in combination.

Most important of all:

THE RISK INCREASES WITH THE NUMBER OF PARTNERS.

Vaginal intercourse without a condom

If a man is infected, the virus present in his ejaculated semen may enter the woman's bloodstream through the vagina. Indeed, even the clear pre-ejaculatory fluid from the man's Cowper's glands may contain the virus.

It also seems possible, although less likely, that the viruses present in a woman's vaginal secretions infect the man by somehow entering his bloodstream through the penis, especially if it has some skin abrasions.

Therefore: Any vaginal intercourse without a condom is unsafe.

Anal intercourse without a condom

Anal intercourse without a condom poses an especially serious risk of infection, because it often involves minor, hardly noticeable tears and other internal injuries. Infected semen should therefore never be ejaculated into the rectum. In fact, it is a major source of infection by the AIDS virus.

Oral intercourse

Licking or sucking the sex organs may also lead to transmission of the AIDS virus from one sexual partner to another, since there is an exchange of bodily fluids involved.

Sucking the penis (fellatio)

Swallowing semen containing the virus must be considered unsafe, because it could enter the bloodstream through even very slight abrasions in the mouth.

Licking or sucking the female sex organs (cunnilingus)

The AIDS virus may also be present in vaginal secretions and thus could possibly lead to infection through cuts, wounds or abrasions in the mouth of a man who ingests them. The danger is apparently not as great as that posed by swallowing semen. However, it is only prudent to consider it risky, too.

Fisting

Inserting the fist and/or the arm into the rectum ("fisting" or "fistfucking") is very risky, even without AIDS. However, the possible tears or other internal injuries likely to occur with this practice make it extremely dangerous if the AIDS virus is present. Even well-scrubbed hands often have slight cuts, bruises and abrasions, and thus a transmission of the virus would be very easy.

In principle, this is also true of vaginal fisting!

Rimming

Licking the anus ("anilingus" or "rimming") is also extremely unsafe, because, if the AIDS virus is present in fecal residue, it could easily be ingested. Moreover, rimming is also the way many other diseases and intestinal disorders are transmitted. These, in turn, can considerably weaken the body and make it more susceptible to an AIDS virus infection.

Drinking urine

Since the AIDS virus has also been found in urine, it is clear that drinking urine is very unsafe, as is any oral contact with any excretions. This is also true of mere skin contact, if the skin is broken or injured in any way.

Sharing sex toys

As long as dildos, vibrators and similar sex toys are used by one and the same person, they obviously pose no risk of infection. However, they become unsafe when they are shared, because one of the users may carry the AIDS virus, which then could be transmitted through the toy to another person. Sex toys should therefore never be shared.

Blood contact

Men and women engaging in S/M (sadomasochistic practices) must take special precautions to avoid any contact with the partner's blood, because it may contain the AIDS virus.

This means not only direct bodily contact with the blood, but also indirect contact through bloody toys, whips, ropes etc.

Needless to say, the same goes for any other possibly infected bodily fluid.

POSSIBLY SAFE

Once we recognize that the AIDS virus is transmitted through bodily fluids, and that any exchange of these fluids during sex is therefore unsafe, we can consider various ways of reducing the risk.

Even some otherwise "unsafe" sexual practices can be made safer.

Every man and woman has to decide for himself or herself if the risk is worth it in any given situation. Still, it is useful to list—and think about—the "possibly safe" sexual practices individually.

SOME OTHERWISE "UNSAFE" SEX CAN BE MADE SAFER.

"Possibly safe" sex is safe in exact proportion to our efforts. It is unsafe in exact proportion to our carelessness.

The precautions listed here therefore have to be taken very seriously and applied very conscientiously in order to achieve a real reduction of risk.

And, of course, the fewer sexual partners we have, the smaller the risk to begin with:

THE RISK DECREASES WITH THE NUMBER OF PARTNERS.

The most important elements that can make otherwise "unsafe" sex somewhat less risky are condoms and certain spermicides and lubricants. Their use does not guarantee complete safety—the practices listed here remain only "possibly safe" or "possibly unsafe"—but in general, condoms and spermicides can and will play an important role in reducing the risk of infection with the AIDS virus.

Condoms

Since a condom catches a man's ejaculated semen, it does prevent the exchange of this particular bodily fluid from one person to another. We also know that the AIDS virus is not smaller than other viruses—such as the herpes virus—for example, that cannot penetrate latex. Indeed, air and water molecules, which are about 1000 times smaller than the AIDS virus, cannot penetrate a condom.

We therefore have reason to believe that a condom offers protection against infection by ejaculated semen. Still, at this time, this is not a scientifically proven fact, only a very reasonable assumption. For this reason, condom use is considered only "possibly safe," not absolutely safe, particularly since condoms are often used incorrectly.

For the correct use of a condom, please remember these points:

- Always use new condoms.
- Keep a ready supply of condoms where they cannot be damaged by moisture or heat.
- Never "test" a condom by blowing it up.
- Put a dab of lubricant into the tip of the condom. This will increase sensation and prevent an air bubble from forming which could perhaps cause the condom to break.

- Put the condom on the fully erect penis and roll it down all the way to the bottom of the shaft.
- Generously lubricate the vaginal entrance or the anus before entry.
- Use only water-soluble lubricant. Oil-based lubricants such as Vaseline or Crisco can damage the condom.
- Upon withdrawal, hold tightly onto the base of the condom. Make sure it does not slip.
- After use, throw the condom away.

Spermicides and lubricants

Many spermicides and some lubricants contain a mild detergent called "nonoxynol-9," which can easily kill the AIDS virus in a lab dish. Whether it can do so inside a human body is not yet clear. On the other hand, we do know that it kills not only sperm cells but also all kinds of other organisms, such as amoebas, the herpes virus, and the bacteria that causes gonorrhea and syphilis. In short, nonoxynol-9 offers very good protection against sexually transmitted diseases, and there is a reasonable hope that it will also work against the AIDS virus.

Still, at this time, there is not enough scientific evidence to prove its effectiveness against the AIDS virus when used inside the human body, and it is also still unclear whether it can safely be used inside the rectum.

Nevertheless, its vaginal use has been quite common for some time and can therefore be strongly recommended together with the use of a condom in order to make vaginal intercourse at least "possibly safe."

It also pays to look around for a lubricant containing "nonoxynol-9," which can reduce the risk of infection even further.

French kissing

French kissing, also called deep kissing or tongue kissing, cannot be considered completely safe, although, so far, there is no known case of anyone having caught the AIDS virus this way.

On the other hand, it may be impossible to prove that someone became infected through deep kissing, because people who kiss this way usually also go on to even more intimate contact.

We do know that the AIDS virus has been found in saliva, although in very low concentrations. An infection through kissing is therefore not very likely. Still, if one of the partners carries the virus and the other one suffers from bleeding gums or even slight other injuries inside the mouth, there could be danger.

It seems wise, therefore, to consider very long and intimate deep kisses to be somewhat risky.

Oral intercourse with precautions

While oral intercourse without any precautions is definitively unsafe, it can be made safer with some effort.

Precautions when sucking the penis

One way of reducing the risk of infection is to avoid swallowing semen, i.e., stop before an ejaculation can occur (*fellatio interrupta*). Actually, one should avoid swallowing even the clear pre-ejaculatory fluid from the man's Cowper's glands.

Another and better way is to suck the penis only after it has been thoroughly covered by a condom. The taste of the condom may take some getting used to, and, of course, one must be careful not to damage it with one's teeth.

Perhaps some manufacturer will, in time, produce condoms with a special selection of agreeable tastes.

Precautions when licking the female sex organs

Using spermicides containing nonoxynol-9 in and around the vaginal opening or licking it through the covering of a dentist's dam may be an option for some men. (Dentist's dams are thin, small rubber sheets available at dentist's supply stores.)

Whether or how any of these precautions work for a particular couple can obviously be decided only through some testing and experimentation.

Vaginal intercourse with a condom and spermicide

Vaginal intercourse should be rather safe, if the man uses a condom correctly and the woman uses a spermicide containing nonoxynol-9.

This double precaution definitively reduces the risk of infection, and it is therefore strongly recommended whenever the partners cannot be completely certain that neither of them carries the virus.

Both condoms and spermicides are easily obtained in drug stores without a prescription, and thus there is no excuse for not using them for protection.

Anal intercourse with condom

Generally speaking, using a condom in anal intercourse does not offer quite the same protection as in vaginal intercourse.

Because the anus is usually tighter than the vagina, the condom may slip or break more easily, and it is not quite clear yet whether spermicides containing nonoxynol-9 can be safely used inside the rectum.

Nevertheless, a lubricant containing nonoxynol-9 should be used and can further reduce the risk.

Of course, one should never use the same condom for both anal and vaginal intercourse. Men who switch from one to the other must change condoms in between.

Urine on unbroken skin

As long as urine comes in external contact only with unbroken skin, there should be no risk of infection.

However, it is sometimes difficult to be certain that the skin is intact everywhere. Slight cuts, bruises or pimples are easily overlooked.

Men and women playing with urine ("golden showers"), even if only externally, therefore need to be especially careful.

SAFE

Any sexual contact which avoids even the possibility of an exchange of bodily fluids poses a very low risk of infection or is actually risk free.

"Safe sex" requires open communication between the partners, some self-control and a great deal of imagination, but it does not have to be dull.

For some, it may also require a drastic re-evaluation of their sexual attitudes and beliefs. For example, many men and women have negative feelings about masturbating in the presence of sexual partners or being masturbated by them. However, when they consider the alternatives of "unsafe" sexual contact, they may find it a little easier to make the necessary adjustment. There is nothing shameful about wanting to protect each other from infection. Moreover:

SAFE SEX CAN BE FUN.

The possibilities listed here are not exhaustive. With cooperation and imagination, men and women can develop their own individual "safe sex" patterns. Indeed, they should tell themselves and each other again and again:

USE YOUR IMAGINATION!

Dry kissing

Social kissing or dry kissing even between lovers does not pose a risk of infection, because there is no exchange of saliva (which could contain the virus).

This is also true of kissing any other part of the body, except, of course, the anus, the vaginal opening and the tip of the penis. However, the neck, the breast, the back, the buttocks, the thighs, the armpits, etc. can be kissed without any fear of infection as long as the skin is intact.

Hugging

Hugging and holding someone close is one of the most important ways of showing affection, and it is completely safe.

Lovers who hug each other and hold each other when falling asleep can develop the intimacy they need in order to explore all their options. Prolonged closed contact like this can be very erotic.

Massage

All kinds of massage are safe that do not directly involve the sex organs. Slow, erotic "body rubs" can be very soothing or stimulating, depending on the partners and the situation.

Massaging the head, neck, back, arms, legs, and feet can create powerful sexual feelings. It can even, in some cases, restore seemingly lost sexual responses. This is why sex therapists have long recommended a deliberate exploration of the body through massage.

This kind of massage, which requires no special skill, only patience, attention and verbal feedback, has been called "sensate focus," because it helps couples to focus on the different sensations they feel in different parts of their bodies as they are stroked, caressed, and touched in various ways.

Such caresses can also be very exciting when soft fur gloves or feathers are used in touching the skin. Different lotions and lubricants also create different sensations.

If the genital area is touched by hand, a lubricant containing nonoxynol-9 may be useful and prevent any possible risk.

For truly devoted and adventurous couples it may be useful to attend some special classes in erotic massage, where they are offered, or to buy one or several massage books for study and exploration.

Body-to-body rubbing

There are many ways in which men and women can rub against each other's bodies. Some have been known as "dry humping," others as "frottage," and they may even lead to orgasm in one or both partners.

Obviously, there is no danger of infection as long as no bodily fluids are exchanged. Even if the man should ejaculate, there need be no risk as long as the semen does not come in contact with any orifice or cut or break in the skin. Here again, a lubricant containing nonoxynol-9 can be useful. Thus, the man may ejaculate on the woman's back or between her breasts.

Women may also reach orgasm by "riding" a man's thigh or forearm and in still other ways.

Body-to-body rubbing is therefore a very attractive and satisfying sexual option.

Mutual masturbation

In the past, mutual masturbation has often been condemned or at least ridiculed as "immature" or embarrassing. However, many women have always depended on being masturbated by their male partners, even during intercourse, if they wanted to reach orgasm.

It is now time to get rid of the prejudice against masturbation and to accept it as a major, wonderful way of giving and receiving sexual pleasure.

Men and women can take turns masturbating each other or they do it simultaneously.

In either case they should use a water-soluble lubricant containing nonoxynol-9 in order to minimize any accidental risk.

It is very important that each of the partners tell the other exactly and very clearly how they want to be masturbated. Everybody needs a slightly different technique, which is impossible to guess. It must be explained to a sexual partner, and thus mutual masturbation becomes a very important means of achieving close communication and complete intimacy.

It also greatly reduces stress and performance anxiety. After all, masturbation in itself feels good. There is no absolute need to reach orgasm, but when desired, the partners can take over from each other and easily reach orgasm on their own.

It is very possible that this open, liberated form of sexual contact comes as an emotional relief to many couples and even increases and enlivens their sex lives. Men especially may find themselves sexually invigorated with their female partners once the old inhibitions have fallen. Women, on the other hand, may reach orgasm just as often or even more through masturbation by their male partners.

Exhibitionism and Voyeurism with consent

Couples who have learned to shed their inhibitions through mutual masturbation, may also learn to enjoy "showing off" to each other or simply watching the other reach orgasm.

Men and women who like the idea can easily create very imaginative and elaborate performances, from a "strip tease" to pretending ignorance about being observed. They can allow themselves to be "caught in the act" or invent drawn-out complicated scenarios in order to increase their mutual excitement.

Some couples also watch "porno-videos" together and watch each other masturbating at the same time.

There is almost no limit to the ways of mutual visual stimulation, and thus this form of absolutely risk-free sexual contact may bcome a major source of satisfaction for many couples.

Telephone sex

Men and women who have come to an appropriate understanding can also call each other on the telephone and thus stimulate each other while masturbating at the same time.

If a certain time is set aside for this, each partner can look forward to the call all day, create a comfortable atmosphere and then enjoy a long session.

This absolutely risk-free form of sexual contact has lately become so popular that many new companies offer the service commercially. Customers pay by credit card. Whatever one might think about this commercial version of the "obscene phone call," one thing is certain: There is no way anyone can catch the AIDS virus through the telephone. Each telephone sex call is one possible infection that did not happen.

S/M without bruising or bleeding

Men and women who like sado-masochistic practices, including bondage, can easily make their sexual encounters risk-free by avoiding any exchange of bodily fluids as well as bruises, cuts or bleeding from any other source.

In fact, the highly ritualistic character of an S/M scene can more easily be changed in the direction of safer sex than many other sexual encounters. Sexual plays of dominance or submission do not depend on the insertion of the penis into the mouth, vagina or anus, and thus S/M couples who are used to working out their scenes in advance have a better chance than many other men and women of finding "safe" sexual alternatives.

Separate sex toys

A couple may want to keep separate sets of HIS and HERS sex toys, which they can use on themselves or each other.

The point is that the sets remain separate and are never shared. However, as long as each partner uses his or her set separately, even in the presence of the other, it can greatly enrich some relationships.

Vibrators of various kinds and dildos can be real "turn ons." Only keep in mind that HIS vibrators and dildos should be used only on him, and HERS only on her.

Living by the Guidelines

Looking at the "safer sex" guidelines, some men and women may wonder whether they really can apply them in their own lives.

Some of the implied changes may seem too drastic.

However, it may help to remember that they are just that—guidelines—nothing more. They are meant to start everyone thinking about sex in a more deliberate and rational way.

For example, one useful way of reading the guidelines is to ask oneself in every instance: "How can this particular behavior become 'safer,' and how can it become 'less safe'?"

Even behavior that is already "unsafe" can be made more dangerous in many ways, not only by having more different partners.

Conversely, behavior that is only "possibly safe" can be made "safer." It can also be made "less safe."

Finally, even some otherwise "safe" sex can be made unsafe through carelessness.

In other words, the guidelines are not unbending iron rules. They are instead only helpful hints. They appeal to our sense of responsibility. They help us in assessing the various degrees of risk and in negotiating sensible sexual encounters.

In the final analysis, we all have to make our own choices.

The guidelines also appeal to our creativity.

There is never a single, correct solution to all sexual problems, and the danger of infection with the AIDS virus is now a sexual problem that we must try to solve, if possible, without giving up our sex lives.

Of course, the "safe sex" guidelines can work only if they are widely known and accepted.

Everyone should be aware of them, so that it becomes easier to talk about sexual options in the age of AIDS.

AIDS DOES NOT HAVE TO MEAN THE END OF SEX.

Not only that, but "safe sex" can prevent or at least greatly slow down the further spread of the disease and many other sexually transmitted diseases.

LIVING BY THE "SAFE SEX" GUIDELINES IS THE BEST WAY OF FIGHTING AIDS.

How to Negotiate "Safer Sex"

Once we have understood the basic principles of "safer sex," we still must learn to put them into practice.

This may not be easy, for many reasons:

- We don't like to change our habits.
- We assume that "safer sex" will be too complicated.
- We assume that it will not be worth the effort.
- We are embarrassed to do some of the things that are safe.
- We are afraid to talk about "safe sex" with a partner.
- We don't know how to bring up the subject with someone we've just met.
- We don't want others to think that we're "weird" or even sick.

- We feel uncomfortable buying condoms or spermicides.
- We think "safer sex" just isn't romantic.
- We just want to follow our feelings and resent all that advance planning required by "safer sex."
- We are afraid we'll offend our partners by suggesting "safer sex."
- We don't like sex with the lights on.
- We are worried that we might lose our partner.
- We think "safer sex" is only a poor substitute, and we want the "real thing."
- We think "safer sex" is only a compromise, and we want "all or nothing."

All of these feelings are perfectly natural, and our partners have them, too.

However, if we truly care about them (and ourselves), we must somehow find a way to break the ice, talk about "safer sex" openly and, above all, put it into practice.

Indeed, "practice" is the magic word here. "Safer sex" has to be practiced in the double meaning: We have to do it, and we have to rehearse it.

But what could be more fun than practicing something that's both enjoyable and healthy?

Practice also means using our imagination in practical ways to improve our sex lives. Remember:

THE MOST IMPORTANT SEX ORGAN IS THE BRAIN.

Therefore, let's all use our heads to have hot and healthy sex.

First, let's see how we can negotiate "safer sex" with ourselves:

THE "SAFER SEX" TEST

Before every date, give yourself the following test:

SEX I LIKE TO DO (OR MIGHT BE
TALKED INTO):

Check all boxes that apply to you—

☐ Dry kissing
☐ *French kissing*
☐ Massage
☐ Body-to-body rubbing
☐ **Sucking the penis (fellatio)**
☐ **Licking the vulva (cunnilingus)**
☐ Mutual masturbation
☐ **Vaginal intercourse**
☐ *Vaginal intercourse with condom + spermicide*
☐ *Sucking the penis with precautions (fellatio interrupta or condom)*
☐ *Licking the vulva with precautions*
☐ **Rimming (licking the anus)**
☐ **Fisting (inserting the hand into the rectum)**
☐ **Anal intercourse without condom**
☐ *Anal intercourse with condom + spermicidal lubricant*
☐ **Sharing sex toys**
☐ Using own sex toys

☐ **Drinking urine**
☐ *Urine externally on unbroken skin*
☐ Telephone sex
☐ Exhibitionism and voyeurism (with consent)
☐ S/M without bleeding and bruising
☐ **S/M with blood contact**

If you checked any activities that are "unsafe" (**boldface**) or only "possibly safe" (*italic*), you should think again. For a really healthy sex life, restrict yourself to activities that are "safe" (lightface).

NEGOTIATING "SAFE SEX" WITH OTHERS

Once you are quite clear in your own mind about what you are willing to do or not to do, it is much easier to talk about it with others.

It's really not so awfully hard anymore to talk about AIDS prevention, because a lot of sensible people are worried about it; and if they are not, they should be.

In fact, if someone wants to have sex with you, but refuses to discuss AIDS prevention, it is a very good idea to go to bed alone. That someone is definitely a risk, and no sexual encounter is worth getting the AIDS virus. Quite apart from that, the person probably also has a lot of sexual hang-ups that would ruin your relationship anyway.

However, there is a lot you can do before you meet any potential sex partners:

After you have tested yourself, cut out the "safe sex" card on page 75, fold it along the dotted line and put it in your wallet or purse. It will come in handy when you begin to discuss details.

You should also get to know your partners very well as individuals before you get sexually involved with them.

Find out about their background, their possible other sexual relationships, past and present. Find out whether they are easy to talk to, whether they are comfortable discussing sexual details, whether they are flexible in their sexual habits, caring, imaginative, creative.

Above all: Don't get yourself into a situation where "safe sex" cannot be discussed and detailed agreements between you become impossible. This can happen, for example, if you drink alcohol or take drugs. These can greatly impair your judgment and make you do things that you might later regret.

SAFE SEX DOES NOT MIX WITH ALCOHOL OR DRUGS.

However, if you are sober, rational and careful, you will have no trouble meeting the right person and making the right decisions. You will also be able to talk about every detail of "safer sex."

PEOPLE WHO CANNOT TALK ABOUT "SAFE SEX" SHOULD NOT HAVE SEX. PERIOD.

Two conversations

Let's assume a couple has just met and have decided to have sex. Let's further assume that the man is the first to bring up the subject of "safe sex." The conversation could develop like this:

HE: I guess you know that many people are now scared of AIDS. I know I am.

SHE: Are you scared to have sex?

HE: No. But I have learned a lot about AIDS, how it's transmitted and how it's *not* transmitted. You can catch the AIDS virus during sex, but you don't have to catch it, if you know how to protect yourself.

SHE: How?

HE: You can practice "safe sex." You can have sex, but you don't exchange any bodily fluids.

SHE: What do you mean? How can you have sex that way?

HE: Just the usual way, but protected. For example, I now always carry a few condoms with me, if there is a chance I might have sex.

SHE: Well, that sound OK. Does that really protect us?

HE: It's a pretty good start. Of course, it's still better, if you also have some spermicidal foam. It usually has some stuff in it, nonoxynol-9,

72

that gives you added protection. Actually, that stuff also protects you against other forms of VD—even herpes.

SHE: Gee, I have never used spermicides. I'm on the pill.

HE: Well, if you want to be sure and get some later, there is still a lot we can do now without having to worry about AIDS.

SHE: For example?

HE: First, let's..

Get out your "safe sex" card (HERS)!
You can cut it out of page 75, fold it along the perforated line and put it in your wallet like a credit card.

Let's assume another couple wants to have sex. The man shows no awareness of AIDS prevention, so the woman takes the initiative:

SHE: Before we get really involved, let me ask you something.

HE: OK.

SHE: A lot of people now are worried about catching the AIDS virus when they're having sex. Aren't you?

HE: What? AIDS? Do you have AIDS? Or wait a minute! Do you think I got AIDS?

SHE: No. I don't think you or I got AIDS, but the virus has been going around, and some people have it without knowing it. They feel perfectly fine, but they can give it to you without realizing it.

HE: What are you trying to tell me?

SHE: I want to have sex with you, but we should both be careful and have "safe sex."

HE: "Safe sex?" What's that?

SHE: No exchange of bodily fluids! Think about it! Sounds a bit complicated, but it's really not. Look, I have here a whole pack of rubbers for you.

HE: Well, I'll be... Gee, I don't know... I've never used rubbers.

SHE: Come on! Let me put one on you. This can be fun. Just see how you like it. And while I'm doing that, let me tell you some more...

Get out your "safe sex" card (HIS)! (You'll find additional ones in the Appendix.)

HIS and HERS "Safe Sex" Cut-Out Cards

AIDS RISK REDUCTION FOR MEN AND WOMEN

Safe

Dry kissing
Hugging
Massage
Body-to-body rubbing
Mutual masturbation
Exhibitionism and voyeurism (with consent)
Telephone sex
S/M without bruising or bleeding
Separate sex toys

· · · · · · · · · · · · FOLD HERE · · · · · · · · · · · ·

Possibly safe

French kissing
Oral sex with precautions (fellatio interrupta, condom, spermicides)
Vaginal intercourse with condom and spermicide
Anal intercourse with condom and spermicidal lubricant
Urine externally on unbroken skin

Unsafe

Vaginal intercourse without condom
Anal intercourse without condom
Oral sex (fellatio and cunnilingus)
Fisting
Rimming
Drinking urine
Sharing sex toys
Blood contact

Now let's assume two gay men have just met in a bar and are about ready to go home together. However, before they leave, one of them feels he should bring up the subject of "safe sex." The conversation could develop like this:

FIRST: You know, it's been a long time since I have taken anybody home. In fact, I'm even a bit nervous about it.

SECOND: Why?

FIRST: Well, you really turn me on. That's one reason, and the other reason is that I really hope we have a good time.

SECOND: Why shouldn't we?

FIRST: Look. Many of my friends are scared to meet anybody new because they're scared of AIDS. I'm not because I know how to protect myself.

SECOND: I'm really glad you're saying that because I've also been worrying about it but I know all about "safe sex." I wouldn't do anything else anyway. So you see, I'm really glad I met you because I know we're really going to have a good time.

Let's assume two other gay men have just met and have decided to go home together. This could be the conversation:

FIRST: Before we leave here, I'd like to ask you something.

SECOND: Okay.

FIRST: Have you seen these "safe sex" cards that are lying around here in the bar? (He gets out one of the "safe sex" cards.)

SECOND: Sure. I don't think anybody is paying attention to them.

FIRST: Are you?

SECOND: No. I think they're ridiculous. Look, either you get it or you don't. I don't believe what these medical people are trying to sell us. They don't know what they're talking about.

FIRST: Have you ever gotten VD?

SECOND: Only once, a long time ago. It's no big deal. I'm perfectly healthy and always have been. I'm not going to let AIDS ruin my sex life.

FIRST: You know, I had a friend just like you who died this summer of AIDS. I don't want my sex life ruined either and therefore I've decided to have only "safe sex."

SECOND: Oh, come on. All that rubber stuff. That's not my style.

FIRST: Gee, I guess I better wait with you. I hope I see you again sometime when you change your thinking about it.

SECOND: Okay. See you around.

Especially for Teens

Sexual interest, curiosity, arousal and desire are hallmarks of adolescence. Although some teens are more sexual than others, both boys and girls have sexual desires and must make decisions about sexual opportunities and options. Sexual feelings are normal and natural. They are wonderful and scary. There are many things to learn about sex if you want it to be a totally positive experience for you and your partner.

Some teens have sex and worry about it later, and some worry about it so much they hardly ever have it; but most boys and girls think and worry about sex a lot. One of the worries is about sexually transmitted disease, and the disease that is most feared is AIDS. A part of the fear is that scientists don't know very much about it yet, and so we are all encouraged to be extra careful about our sexual choices.

You have probably heard a lot about AIDS and may even know someone who has it or has died from it. Certainly, everyone knows who Rock Hudson was, but you may not have known that he was homosexual. Many men who enjoy sex with other men do not tell anyone else about it. Many men who enjoy sex with women also enjoy sex with men and do not tell their female partners. This creates a problem for girls and women who want to avoid exposure to the AIDS virus, because homosexual men are a high risk group. You may have heard that women do not get AIDS. That is not true. It is true that more men than women get AIDS and scientists are not yet sure why.

PEOPLE AT RISK FOR AIDS

1. Homosexual and bisexual men (keeping in mind that the bisexual men are much more numerous than the exclusively homosexual men).
2. Intravenous drug users sharing needles.
3. The sexual partners of people in these first groups.
4. The sexual partners of these partners; and
5. Children conceived, born and nursed by infected mothers.

It is important to realize that you can catch the AIDS virus by sharing a contaminated hypodermic needle or through sexual contact. A baby can be infected by a mother with AIDS virus during pregnancy or while nursing. If you catch the AIDS virus, you may or may not get AIDS, but you can pass the virus to others. The only way to know if you have the AIDS virus is through a blood test.

> You cannot tell if a person has the AIDS virus by looking at them, by knowing them or by their assurance that they don't have it.

There is no way for you to know about the other person, so you must protect yourself. Not sharing needles is pretty easy for most teens, because most don't inject drugs; but sexual contact presents a problem, because most teens are sexual with a partner in some way. It is unrealistic to imagine that people will not be sexual, so it is important to learn to practice safe sex to avoid all sexually transmitted diseases.

> Safe sex is better sex

because you don't have to worry.

> Intercourse and oral sex with a condom are safe.

Exchange of body fluids is risky.

> Hugging—holding—caressing and masturbation are safe with anyone.

Intercourse and oral sex with many partners is risky.

Kissing is safe.

French kissing is theoretically considered risky, even though there is no known case of anyone catching the AIDS virus in this way.

Some Important Precautions for Teens

1. Don't have sex while drunk or high. Sex is its own high. When you drink or take drugs, your judgment is impaired and your decisions are not based in reality.
2. Don't be persuaded to have unsafe sex because you want to please your partner. Sexual feelings in adolescence are often experienced as an urgent need for release and satisfaction. Demands and ultimatums are sometimes used to convince a potential partner to have sex.
3. Don't feel you have to make a forced choice between intercourse and oral sex. You can offer a safe sex alternative.
4. Take responsibility for sex if you plan to have it or think you might. Boys and girls should always carry condoms even if they practice another form of birth control.

5. Don't be blackmailed into unsafe sex to save a relationship. Respect yourself even if your partner does not respect you.

REMEMBER

AIDS virus is passed only through very intimate contact, exchange of body fluids and contaminated needles. People do not catch the AIDS virus through casual social contact. You need not fear

1. Food prepared by persons with AIDS virus
2. Beauty or barber shop services
3. Touching friends or relatives
4. Health care procedures
5. Blood transfusions, which are now tested and safe

It is important to be responsible about sex, and it is important to continue to feel positive about your own sexual sharing with a partner of your choice. Sex-negative forces have always tried to make people fear and/or feel guilty about their natural, normal, sexual feelings and behavior.

Appendix

SAFE SEX PRODUCTS AND WHERE TO GET THEM

It is a sad commentary on the sex attitudes in our society that many AIDS education programs have been "put on hold" so as not to offend the political sensibilities of the anti-sexual groups that equate sexual ignorance with innocence.

Fortunately, the makers of sex products started three years ago to commission new product designs and testing for SAFE SEX. Many new products are now ready for distribution.

The Institute is aware that there may be many fine products available that we do not know about. We can only recommend products that we have evaluated. The products listed below adhere to the specifications the Institute has set.

FORPLAY PRODUCTS (with nonoxynol-9):

ForPlay Sensual Lubricant
ForPlay Rub Down
ForPlay Adult Toy Cleaner

PREPAIR PRODUCTS (with nonoxynol-9)

Personal Lubricant
Personal Lubricant with Applicator
Contraceptive Gel with Applicator

The condom recommendations made by Dr. Clark Taylor, senior researcher of SAFE SEX products for The Institute for Advanced Study of Human Sexuality are as follows:

* PLAY SAFE--lubricated with nonoxynol-9, very strong, medium sized with instructions for use and safe sex guidelines by the San Francisco AIDS Foundation in Spanish and English.

* PRIME--lubricated with nonoxynol-9, very strong, 8" long, regular width.

* GOLD CIRCLE COIN--non-lubricated, odorless, tasteless, large size.

* CHAPEAU "39"--lubricated, ribbed, extra wide.

* CHAPEAU BLACKY--lubricated, black color, reservoir tip, tapered.

* YAMABUKI #3--same as above but with fine ribbing for extra pleasure.

* HUGGER CONDOMS--lubricated, smaller diameter, medium length, strong.

FOUR "SAFE SEX" VIDEOTAPES:

1. "Norma and Tony--Safe Sex for High Risk Bisexuals."
2. "Erotic Safe Sex--A documentary for Heterosexuals."
3. Erotic Safe Sex for Gay and Bi Males--A Documentary"
4. "How to Have a J.O. Party."

SAFE SEX KIT--Everything You Need for Hot, Healthy Sex: A personal sampler of recommended SAFE SEX items.

For information call or write:

In the U.S.: The Institute for Advanced Study of Human Sexuality, 1523 Franklin Street, San Francisco 94109, Phone 415-928-1133.

In Canada: A.P. Research, Ltd., Box 200 Postal Station A, Vancouver, B.C., Canada, Phone 604-669-5404

HIS and HERS "Safe Sex" Cut-Out Cards

AIDS RISK REDUCTION FOR MEN AND WOMEN

Safe

Dry kissing
Hugging
Massage
Body-to-body rubbing
Mutual masturbation
Exhibitionism and voyeurism (with consent)
Telephone sex
S/M without bruising or bleeding
Separate sex toys

• • • • • • • • • • • FOLD HERE • • • • • • • • • • • •

Possibly safe

French kissing
Oral sex with precautions (fellatio interrupta, condom, spermicides)
Vaginal intercourse with condom and spermicide
Anal intercourse with condom and spermicidal lubricant
Urine externally on unbroken skin

Unsafe

Vaginal intercourse without condom
Anal intercourse without condom
Oral sex (fellatio and cunnilingus)
Fisting
Rimming
Drinking urine
Sharing sex toys
Blood contact

HIS and HERS "Safe Sex" Cut-Out Cards

AIDS RISK REDUCTION FOR MEN AND WOMEN

Safe

Dry kissing
Hugging
Massage
Body-to-body rubbing
Mutual masturbation
Exhibitionism and voyeurism (with consent)
Telephone sex
S/M without bruising or bleeding
Separate sex toys

• • • • • • • • • • •FOLD HERE • • • • • • • • • • •

Possibly safe

French kissing
Oral sex with precautions (fellatio interrupta, condom, spermicides)
Vaginal intercourse with condom and spermicide
Anal intercourse with condom and spermicidal lubricant
Urine externally on unbroken skin

Unsafe

Vaginal intercourse without condom
Anal intercourse without condom
Oral sex (fellatio and cunnilingus)
Fisting
Rimming
Drinking urine
Sharing sex toys
Blood contact

HIS and HERS "Safe Sex" Cut-Out Cards

AIDS RISK REDUCTION FOR MEN AND WOMEN

Safe

Dry kissing
Hugging
Massage
Body-to-body rubbing
Mutual masturbation
Exhibitionism and voyeurism (with consent)
Telephone sex
S/M without bruising or bleeding
Separate sex toys

· · · · · · · · · · FOLD HERE · · · · · · · · · ·

Possibly safe

French kissing
Oral sex with precautions (fellatio interrupta, condom, spermicides)
Vaginal intercourse with condom and spermicide
Anal intercourse with condom and spermicidal lubricant
Urine externally on unbroken skin

Unsafe

Vaginal intercourse without condom
Anal intercourse without condom
Oral sex (fellatio and cunnilingus)
Fisting
Rimming
Drinking urine
Sharing sex toys
Blood contact